T0006919

Optic Nerve

Optic Nerve

poems

MATTHEW HOLLETT

Brick Books

Library and Archives Canada Cataloguing in Publication

Title: Optic nerve / Matthew Hollett.
Names: Hollett, Matthew, 1982- author.
Identifiers: Canadiana (print) 20220489637 | Canadiana (ebook) 20220489688 |
ISBN 9781771315999 (softcover) | ISBN 9781771316002 (EPUB) |
ISBN 9781771316019 (PDF)
Classification: LCC PS8615.O4373 O68 2023 | DDC C811/.6—dc23

We gratefully acknowledge the Canada Council for the Arts, the Government of
Canada through the Canada Book Fund, and the Ontario Arts Council for their
support of our publishing program.

Edited by Barry Dempster and Sue Sinclair.
Author photo by April White.
The cover image is a detail of the lithograph *Puddles* by Jon McNaught.
The book is set in Kepler.
Design by Marijke Friesen.
Printed and bound by Coach House Printing.

Brick Books
487 King St. W.
Kingston, ON
K7L 2X7
www.brickbooks.ca

Though much of the work of Brick Books takes place on the ancestral lands of the
Anishinaabeg, Haudenosaunee, Huron-Wendat, and Mississaugas of the Credit
peoples, our editors, authors, and readers from many backgrounds are situated
from coast to coast to coast in Canada on the traditional and unceded territories of
over six hundred nations who have cared for Turtle Island from time immemorial.
While living and working on these lands, we are committed to hearing and return-
ing the rightful imaginative space to the poetries, songs, and stories that have been
untold, under-told, wrongly told, and suppressed through colonization.

CONTENTS

In Camera

In Negative

In Print

In Camera

Cloudlarking

I'm halfway up Duckworth when the guillotine
gives way, veering mercifully east, a dull blade of vapour
scraping razor-burnt sky. It macerates and sinks,
billows over the Narrows like a burial shroud,
then frays, cocoons, and transfigures itself: an embryo
pluming upwards from an umbilical tail, a tadpole, a codfish,
a humpback whale. Cresting the hill by the Battery Hotel,
I watch the leviathan straddle the far side of the harbour
on a billion spindly tentacles, and imagine my front window
speckling with suckermarks as it gams and pastures. Huffing up
Gibbet Hill, I discover the rest of its herd grazing the Southside
and the suburbs, licking crusted road salt, waggling underbellies,
inking new territories. The first drop dampens my camera
just as I pass another photographer heading down; I nod at him
and he nods at the clouds and says: *It's something to work with.*

A Profusion of Handsome Japanese Papers

A hangnail of plastic beckoned from the wrapper,
irresistible as the pull-cord dangling at the bottom
of my grandparents' basement stairs. *Pull here,*
the package should have read, *to open*
a new age in space exploration, to open Beethoven's
Fifth Symphony, to open hostilities. I pulled.
Five hundred species of paper spilled
from a plastic chrysalis, and every shadow in a small radius
leapt for the nearest corner to quiver there,
hissing. Diamonds upon diamonds
of chiyogami improvised a fireworks competition
on my desk, like wildflowers
forced through a pencil sharpener, like capelin rolling
in the glitter of a discothèque. *Pull here,*
it should have said, *to begin your career*
as a lepidopterist, a pyrotechnician, a capital letter
in an illuminated manuscript. Leaning close, my eyes struck
oil skimmed from a moonlit pond, a medieval tapestry
writhing with maggots, a pulped treasury
of Calvin & Hobbes. *The publisher didn't use the proper*
print fixative. Needless to say, when I picked up the book,
all the letters slid off the pages
in a heap of gibberish. I've somehow come into possession
of Calvin's palimpsest: here's a cartoon fistfight
bristling with exclamation points, here's a colony of bees
engulfing a pachinko machine, here's twenty years
scraped off a painter's studio floor, here's a Bridget Riley

locking eyes with a Hokusai in the MoMA
just before the doors close. Here's where I drove off a bridge
and a Portuguese man o' war hit the windshield,
here's the taste of gasoline
distilled into nine square inches, here's a nautical map
of the moon. *Mare Cognitum. Mare Insularum.*
When Mare Moscoviense was proposed by the Soviet Union,
it was only accepted with the justification
that Moscow is a state of mind. Did you even read
the history chapter I assigned? Here's the sound of snow
falling on the ocean, here's the lindy hop from *Hellzapoppin'*
reenacted by chrysanthemums, here's an artist's impression
of how an octopus sees its garden. *Pull here*
for altered thinking processes, closed- and open-eye visuals,
synesthesia, an altered sense of time, and
spiritual experiences. Here's Calvin urinating on
Your Text Here, here's a strip of tiny squares
with Cheshire smiles, here's a monarch wing
magnified fifteen times, here's
where I closed my eyes.

After André Kertész's *A Bird Market near the Hôtel de Ville,
Paris, 1926*

Nine thin lines, tight as guitar strings
bind the bird inside its miniature
cage, a balsa-wood chamber
that resonates in your hands

without a sound. The vendor runs his finger
along the bars. *I cannot make the bird sing
now*, he intones, *but for soixante francs
it will sing to your children*

at first light. It isn't his pitch, but the canary's
heartbeat thrumming the walls
that persuades you. Still, you hold the box
with your fingertips, a certain distance from your chest,

as if it's wired to explode. Wasn't it
just yesterday you were shown one of those
newfangled rangefinders, squinting
at dials, listening to its clicks,

fretting at how fragile the world became
in its prism? Your thumbs are so clumsy, and you couldn't help
but imagine the roll of film coiled inside, so
tightly wound, so sensitive to light,

so terrified.

Roll Over

We didn't learn the burned-out building had been a cinema
until the day they tore it down, but we squeezed into the crowd
to watch an excavator pulverize it into popcorn. In the rubble

we dug slivers of film like mussels, blowing ash off newsreels, musicals,
porn. I uncoiled a strip of colour, a cartoon beagle spinning through
a wild blue yonder. He was a runaway load of laundry, an adorable

ouroboros pinwheeling into a yin-yang of yellow and brown,
balled up like yarn or a yoga instructor. By yo-yoing the filmstrip
on my finger, I trained him to somersault at half speed, or double,

and when I took him home he curled up in a film canister. I clipped
the mangled ends from his reel, so now when I take him out for a tumble
he isn't scorched or torn when it ends. He just *goes*, like a bubble.

Prisoner's Cinema

Close your eyes. Imagine them as twin incisions
in your skin. Their extremities, where your eyelids crimp,
act as a kind of hinge. Have you ever looked closely
at how wings attach to an insect? Or at the shutter mechanism
in a single lens reflex? When the mirror in your camera flips
and the viewfinder goes black, your eyeballs squirm and fidget
in that empty theatre where every unconscious hour
is spent waiting for a projectionist to get his act together. Even awake,
your eyelids flutter like shutter-happy tourists—if you could play back
every blink and blackout, days would flicker past
in time-lapse, followed by hours of bedroom walls convulsing
with rapid eye movement. This is the dim unmopped lobby in the
cinema of your dreams, the dark side of the moon of your brain.
Close your eyes again, this time imagining an astronaut's visor,
a thin gold membrane between you and oblivion. Now press
lightly on the sides of your eyelids. Do you see colours? Static?
Outer space? Can you make out shadows of shadows in a cave?

Some Kind of Understanding (1)

January air shimmers
with the querulous babble
of feathered apples.

—

Is this serrated serenade a froggelhorn
with a flu in its throat? A car alarm
gone hoarse and buggy? Oh, crows.

—

Some birds sing. A blackbird rewires
dials on its syrinxthesizer, circuit-bends
a whistle through a woodchipper.

Moss

squats. It shambles into shadows
that no one was using, mooches
a shabby mattress from the underbrush,
metastasizes. Sylvia Plath's
So many of us! So many of us!
is a motto it mumbles
softly, its mouths full
of upholstery tacks
as it retrofits forest floor
into thrift-store sofa. It repeats
itself, repeats itself. Chintzy,
moss dismisses frivolities
like flowers and seeds, doesn't take root
or take shape, only barely takes
hold. Unbeholden, unbeheld,
it plays dormant, pretends to let you
walk all over it, then sinks
its gums in, a welcome mat
gone feral.

Trip the Light Domestic

Light lives in tiny houses
and never locks its doors: a drop of water,
a sliver of glass, the glint of an eye. Light
likes company dropping by at any hour.
It knows a trick or two, how to set a table

while your back is turned. In Bonne Bay
in late September, light labours to keep the day
long, sweeping the hardwood horizon, burnishing
brass hills, mopping the linoleum pond. After dinner
light shoos our kayaks further out the fjord

and turns in for a snooze, soon re-emerging
to sashay behind our paddles, glimmery-eyed,
in the glow of plankton's bioluminescent swoon.
Light won't be fooled, packs a pocketful of
self-defence moves, likes to keep an eye on you.

Wind in St. John's

The wind in St. John's snorts saltwater
in the parking lot by Cabot Tower before cannonballing
down Signal Hill Road as if it's spotted its house
on fire from afar. It side-swipes a police car
and an officer radios *wind northeast sixty*
kilometres an hour gusting to eighty, changing to north seventy
fishtailing to ninety down Duckworth. The wind in St. John's
hefts clouds like Rambo shoulders ammunition belts.
It cranks up, crumples beer cans in its fists, pisses its initials
in the snow outside the courthouse. Police sirens
goose-chase its trail of sideways seagulls, missing
shingles, puddles slinking uphill. The dispatcher crackles
same goddamn nor'easter blustering seventy down New Gower,
shit-disturbing to ninety by midnight, probably gut-rotted
to forty by morning. The wind in St. John's
doesn't have time for this shit. It's got car alarms
to serenade, construction sites to plunder,
trash to kick down Kenmount. It snaps bras
from clotheslines, shreds power lines like electric
guitars, snuffs out traffic lights. The wind in St. John's
never could sit still. It spun its wheels in Wreckhouse,
blew into town for a gig tossing recyclables off the cliff
at Cape Spear. The wind in St. John's resents its reputation,
all the wind warnings and special weather statements. All it wants
is to give everything a whirl. When it gets wound up
it rip-roars back to Cabot Tower, flaunting the horizon
like a prizefighter's belt. Cops love to chase the wind

into international waters, where it idly shuffles waves,
dizzies compasses like roulette wheels, tosses ships
like so many poker chips. A card shark, wind needs to risk its neck
just to breathe. All night it fumes and seethes, bluffing eighty
when it's barely fifty, trying its luck at hundred-and-twenties,
going thirty-for-sixty til four in the morning when it crashes, blurs,
and curls up on a sandbar, outsnoring the foghorns.

Musca Depicta

A riotous still life, oodles of grapes hobnobbing
around a glass of champagne—*To your health!*—as two figs
lech after an indecently halved peach. I can almost see
my reflection, each peel bejewelled with the same prim water-drops
that spangle coke machines. A single fly lurks below the fruit
like the list of side effects in a drug advertisement: *Ask your curator*
if musca depicta is right for you! Nine out of ten
recommend coming to terms with the certainty of death
through microdoses of trompe-l'œil insects. Adverse effects
may include headaches, nausea, the urge to lean closer,
and sudden awareness of the futility of pleasure. I hardly need
the reminder, having just emerged from the hushed chambers
of the museum's collection of peat bog cadavers.

Outside, unimpeachable sun takes a sledgehammer
to Dublin. One heat-stricken man grips a lamppost, another
has collapsed on the grass in the park. They shrivelled
in dim vitrines, half-human half-raisin. First responders
respond, ambulance doors thrown wide. I duck inside
a corner store for a bottle of water and an ominous slab
labelled a "fruit slice." I sink into a bench, blisters simmering,
and look up what I'm eating: *A raisin spice pie, also known*
as gur cake, or a flies' graveyard. The one that still had a face
was the hardest to see—his strange ginger hair, his bog-gnawed ear,
his fruit-leather cheeks. Around me, couples nuzzle and swoon.
Leaves so languorous they drizzle. I feel my own tongue pickling.

Frost

crop-dusts the yard overnight
as if salting the earth. It froths
tall grass into a rollicking snickersnee,
a bajillion icicle-shivs itching to melt
into evidencelessness. Frost is fraught
with the persnickety not-quite-violence
of sandpaper or a plague of locusts.
It laces rotting apples with razor blades,
sharpens the partridgeberries. Up close
it's sharkskin, splintered glass, a crystalline
circuitry of needles and sparks. It's weaponized
spindrift, dew on meth. It wizens the rosebush
beyond all reason, crazes car windows,
re-embroiders the spider's embroidery.
A conspiracy of lickspittles,
frost sabre-rattles, embrittles, glitterbombs,
blights. It gnashes and gloats. At first light,
it has a dream where its teeth fall out.

Wanton Entanglement

Is a spider's web a work of art, or a tool,
or a kind of architecture? When I found one
on a curiosity shop shelf, mounted on black
paper and framed behind glass, I mistook it at first
for a photograph. If a spider's web is an artwork, is it
drawing or sculpture or textile? If the frame had hung
in a gallery, it would've been labelled *Oil on silk*
on paper. Apparently you use spray paint, white or silver,
then hairspray so it sticks to the backing. Sometimes
there are insect wings or single legs stuck to the web,
as if a construction worker's gone to lunch
and left a hammer dangling in the scaffolding, except
more ham sandwich crust than hammer. If a spider's web
is a tool, is it more fishing net or satellite dish,
mousetrap or meathook? If it's architecture, is it more
hammock or hunting blind or torture chamber? Does a fresh
coat of paint and a wooden frame make it more exquisite
or kitsch? Gathering dust and dead flies on a shelf, the web
had become a caricature of itself. It was a bullet hole
in black velvet, a fetal ultrasound of an unborn
vinyl record, origami instructions for folding
a crumpled ball of paper. If a spider's web is a pattern
to follow, a kind of allegory, should we learn from it
the beauty of labour, or the virtues of preparedness
and patience, or to put our trust in bodily fluids
and ephemeral gestures? Is a web a spider's
dragnet, its murder weapon, or merely

the scene of the crime? Is it more burial shroud,
body bag, or chalk outline? Or is it one of those corkboards
on crime-solving dramas, a constellation of mugshots
and surveillance photos and string, except our detective
just twiddles his spinnerets and waits for a suspect
to crash into the webbing? I couldn't help but wonder
if the web on the shelf had been framed as decor,
or in memoriam, or for murder. From one angle
it diagrammed endless dead ends, from another
the interconnectedness of all things. It was the skeleton
of a small patch of atmosphere, the world's flimsiest kite
lifted carefully from a tree, a stenographer's record
of two branches shooting the breeze. It was a trampoline
for betweenity. What's the tensile strength of metaphor?
Can it snap? Is fastening a line from *this* to *that*
an act of restraint, or of love? The only thing caught
in the spider's web was a sticker that said
$19.99. It was a masterpiece of knickknackery,
a glinting pinwheel with the gravitational pull
of a spiral galaxy. It's stuck with me.

Peer Gynt Peels the Mushrooms

No Kaiser are you; you are naught
but a plastic tub of mushrooms.
I'll peel your cold cling-film curtain
despite your chorus of huddled harrumphs
scolding me to close the fridge door,
drown the lights.

You won't escape,
you gilled dollops, moss-polyps, mud-scallops
dreaming of a forest floor. How dare you
be so dubiously aquatic? A bloom of jellyfish
gone stale, a dapple of whatever sort of tadpoles
metamorphose into moons.

Now, tossed on the grill!
Piddly Hindenburg speech balloons,
you crash-land *hmms* and *uhs* and *ums*—
misfired champagne corks
fizzling with indecisiveness,
muttering away your plumpness with a hiss.

North Head Trail

On a day when the waves are unfurling
and the wind curls around the Battery Hotel
and the shadows of clouds are cartwheeling
down the side of Signal Hill,
oh come for a galefilero,
we'll walk the North Head Trail.

Oh walk with me, oh walk with me,
through the Battery, past the apple trees,
leaning backwards against the wind
to where the houses trail off and the trail begins,

past the crevice where pigeons preen
and wish they were lucky as albatrosses,
to the cliff where seagulls wheel and scream,
drape bedrock with bedsheets of shit and salt,
and sometimes sleep, and sometimes dream
of Ron Hynes singing *St. John's Waltz*.

We'll find a song, we'll find a song
in the whistle of wind as we walk along,
in a plunk in a bucket when a berry drops in,
in the crack and crash of an iceberg collapsing.

The hill catches fire in the autumn
with little red leaves that flicker like candles
and lick at our sandals like fiery tongues.

Wind tumbles them into incandescence
and they glow at the edge of our vision
as the sky burns to embers around us.

Like a dandelion, like a dandelion,
the trail bursts up through rock to find the sun
and blooms into a bright windswept horizon,
so close your eyes and stick your nose in.

Olbers' Paradox, or Sunglasses at Night

Since there are countless stars, the question goes,
why isn't the night sky as glittery as Times Square
times infinity? Olbers wasn't the first to wonder this,
though some prankster taped the paradox to his back
and it stuck. If every line of sight ends in a star,
the night sky should be lustrous as lemon peel,
full moon reduced to fruit sticker. So why, instead,
this lava lampiness of Milky Way and murk?
Why is there darkness? *Suppose the void is so immense*
that no ray from it has yet been able to reach us!
quoth Edgar Allen Poe, earning an asterisk
in the history of astrophysics. As it turns out,
the reason we know *Sunglasses at Night*
as pop song and not ophthalmological advice
is that most stars aren't visible from Earth
because the time it takes their light to arrive
is greater than the age of the universe. Of course,
this is lunacy. If Olbers had only watched Looney Tunes,
he'd've known that enlightenment is a lightbulb flicking on
over your noggin, and all it takes is a falling anvil
(or Newton's apple) to bring stars dervishing.

Entoptic

after Joe Carter's *Longliner Construction, St. Alban's, Bay d'Espoir, Newfoundland*

Peering into the doorway of the eye,
we can observe the diligent vitreous bodies
who change burnt-out rods and cones, polish the dark
side of the lens, and keep the upside-down world turning
right-side-up again. At the moment one worker is neck-deep
in ganglionic gutter, while others set up a projection screen,
scrub away visual clutter, assemble scaffolding. A single bulb
dangles from the optic nerve. It's a highly focussed
discipline, part cave painter, part Buckminster Fuller,
part orb-weaving spider. If you prefer looking through
telescopes backwards, or can play *Blackbird*
from inside a guitar, you should consider applying.

In Negative

Tickling the Scar

In spring the ice on the Lachine Canal melts
into algae blooms and great blue herons. Grackles
and red-winged blackbirds warble urgent duets
with distant ambulances. Thousands of Montrealers
are drowning in their beds. I walk the canal
because I'm grateful to breathe, even through a mask,
and because it feels spacious. Less petri dish. Along the path,
freshly dredged jumbles of crossbars and wheels
are so consumed by zebra mussels that you can barely tell
they used to be bicycles. A survivor of the virus describes
feeling as though a bag of rice were being dropped on her chest
every time she took a breath. Seagulls drop bivalve shells
on the canal's concrete walls, where they split open
into pairs of tiny, desiccated lungs. Whenever I see a single one,
I imagine its partner coughed up on the opposite side of the water.
There are nursing homes where staff have deserted en masse.
A man takes a job at one because it's the only way
to be with his father. He sobs when describing to a reporter
the stench of urine, feces and disinfectant. A rainbow
is painted over its front entrance. At CHSLD Herron,
a relief nurse finds ninety-year-olds so dehydrated
they're unable to speak, *with urine bags full to bursting.*
They bring the army in, repurpose refrigerated trucks
as morgues. Songbirds build nests with discarded masks.
I think of walking the canal as *tickling the scar.*
Tracing a fault line between "before" and "normal."
There was a lake here, before it was torn

into an industrial corridor. A long blue lung.
It's slowly healing over. You can sit on the grass
and watch herons stitch it back together
while your phone shows you horror after horror.
They're reopening the restaurants tomorrow.

Hard Months

March comes in through the nose like a line of blow
and blows out like a lamp. April comes in like
a mouthful of cinnamon. It goes around
like whooping cough and overstays its welcome
while May comes in and goes out and comes in again
like a pigeon on public transportation. Summer stumbles
into September. October curls up in your lap
like an indoor cat. When it gets out by accident,
November comes to town like a monster truck show
and flattens it. November goes moose hunting
and never comes back, and December steps in
like stepping on a Lego brick. It goes gangrenous.
January comes in like a doctor who asks
if you'd like to sit down, goes on and on as the world
glazes over. February comes in on your clothes
like cigarette smoke. It never comes out.

A Beetle Found Drowning

Is it so strange to wake up as an insect? A groggy
Gregor Samsa, wobbling on legs like tangled
coathangers, your sister chasing you out of the house
with a rolled-up newspaper? I tumbled down a hill
into brackish water and my shadow kept falling
and cracked open on barnacled stone. In hot
buttery sunlight it burst like popcorn. I was stuck
in a prism of surface tension as if bubblegummed
to a movie theatre floor. Instead of flashing before
my eyes, my life sputtered like a candle
choking on its own wax. I was a body floating above
its ghost, forced to watch as a bewildering flipbook
of balloon animals flickered in my silhouette,
a family of raccoons trapped in a garbage bag,
a fusillade of inkblot tests. My shadow was a polliwog
oscillating between grasshopper and octopus.
It had wriggled out from the wrong end
of a fountain pen, taught itself to dance
by watching news footage of mushroom clouds
and Elvis. It writhed arabesques on the tidepool
floor, like gut flora trying to invent language.
I was barely above water. Froth corked my throat.
In its impulsive implosive masquerade, my shadow
jigged ransom note after ransom note. When my leg
snagged shore I clawed through surface scrim
as if through a movie screen, squelched out from

that silent film to an audience of one. My tormentor
clung to my every step. The faster I ran, the faster
it clapped. It was enraptured, umbilical, my marionette.

Some Kind of Understanding (2)

Under the snow, white cat hair
caught between paving stones. My hair too,
cut in the backyard during lockdown.

—

Having besqueaked me to the window,
a cardinal discourteously transforms
into a neighbour's clothesline chirruping.

—

Days when my only human contact is this:
squeezing the peel of a clementine
to tell how ripe it is.

Opening Moves

Nothing is so sharp
as the far edge of First Pond in September,
where rusty box-cutter blades of shale
rip the ragged seam of the water,
tear holes in the very fabric of the air.
Look! Just by your ear—a thin blue incision
in the oxygen, a kind of hypoatmospheric

needle. A dragonfly sutures itself
to its reflection, lifts, trembles as if held between
thimble and finger, then lands pointedly
on one reed after another, as if it, and not
some hidden spider, has left
silver filaments labyrinthing space
where flies are likeliest. How can a creature

so miniscule, so picayune
make so many decisions? By the time
we decide where to swim, it's attended
to sixty things. It's maddening. It hones the day's
sharp edges: the barbwire brambles
that prod us to the waterline, our arm-hairs bristling
in the wind off the pond, every atom

of grit in our sandals, and this morning's argument
prickling under our skins. So when you shove me
face-first into the living machinery of the pond,

I understand,
even as my flesh is vivisected
by the mezzaluna sun, my bones
buzz-sawed by mosquitos, and my brain

unravelled by whirligig beetles. I only ask
that you wade in, gather the scraps
of my hair and skin, fragments of teeth, take time
to wind my veins and viscera around twigs,
and toss piece after piece of me back to the beach
to let the darning needles
do their thing.

After David Milne's *Bomb Crater behind Vimy Station, 6 June 1919*

Watercolour, without water
and almost without colour—more newspaper clipping
than painting, a saccade of dry-brushed
scratches and stitches, the hesitations
of an exhausted eye. Yet half the page is unscathed,
as if these scars are all that remains to be seen:
this scrounged-together town the colour
of bandage and bruise, these ruptured brushstrokes
reckoning fences or trenches, this foreground
engulfed by the crater itself—that gaping, unslakeable
baby robin's mouth, that grisly scythe
torqued into the earth, that tarnished
looking-glass with its thousand-yard stare,
that tormented blister rimmed with dried blood
and oozing pus. But what lived here
before? What's that glint of pencil, jutting out
from behind a broken brushstroke? Milne wrote,
A litter of shell fragments, cartridges,
shell cases and dud shells big and little,
helmets and water bottles of three nations,
boots and uniforms, the boots often
with socks and feet in them.
The earth had been
torn up and torn up and torn up again.

Seeing Is Forgetting the Name of the Thing One Sees

Before I knew your name,
your glance glanced mine across a room,

knocked a hairline crack in my brain
that widened with every blink

into a blank that only one word would fill.
I saw you so clearly then.

You cornered me by the wine,
filled me in. I didn't see you again

until a couple of years after
we'd stopped seeing each other,

although I couldn't tell you where
or when. It was just a split-second

glancing through an album of photos
someone else had taken.

I'm Sorry, I Have to Ask You to Leave

I know, I know, I've noticed that myself, the way
the shell of the building glows, like a fire burned down
but not gone out. I think it's streetlights bouncing around
the bare concrete. No, no. If it was up to me I'd let you,

but I'd get in trouble. You have to contact management
if you want to take photos—tons of people show up
with fancy cameras, but it's a liability issue, as you
can imagine. I've taken a few myself—from the twelfth floor

you can see the harbour, both bridges. Before we finished
the fence, some kids snuck in one night and spray-painted
cocks on all the columns, had a romp kicking down three days
of drywall. That's when they started us in the evenings, about

two months ago. I'm Becky, by the way. Oh, I don't mind it here alone—
just look up at those cranes, that blue one only just turned
eight years old, they had her shipped over from the UK,
and the yellow one's from Germany. At night they release the locks

and the ladies, we call them ladies, turn in the wind.
See the way they all point in the same direction? Like
weathervanes, or ballerinas. I've been taking classes
towards my operator's license—imagine sitting up there

this time of night. Or in fog, like a space station. I never minded heights. As soon as I start my shift I head straight up to the twelfth, I call it my lighthouse. Tonight I borrowed my dad's binoculars, these, that's how I saw you.

Shipshape

In Halifax it greets me like a gauntlet of bear traps.
Sidestepping swollen potholes on Quinpool, I pass a traffic island
with its mascara of snow, a bicycle wheel crushed into a taco,
a bird's nest asquint with icicles. Winterized cypresses
bulge from burlap envelopes, beside the overturned hull
of Citadel Hill. A plow's three-point turn leaves curving tracks
that cross themselves like the fish on those bumper stickers.
Twisting symmetry into symbol, my brain Rorschachs
any bent bottlecap into a hieroglyph: two lines
bowing outwards and trussed at the tips, like gunwales
swelling the ribs of a ship. Like pickpocketed ( ) parentheses,
or an eye that wanders off before I can finish drawing it.

With Tongue

Mine won't cloverleaf or even
hot dog bun. Never learned to gleek,
whistle, blow bubblegum, or knot
a maraschino stem. The closest I've come
is licking finger and thumb to snuff out
candle wicks. I've scalded the tip on
gas-station coffee and molten
marshmallow, sandpapered taste buds
on too many postage stamps. In grad school
Josh sculpted a spoon with its bowl a mould
of his, served us conceptual art with it. Catherine
cast everyone's bellybuttons in bronze, and yours
was the cutest. We were advised to read Merleau-Ponty
once to get the gist, twice to comprehend,
three times to understand, which I've found
holds true for more hands-on
phenomenological pursuits. You let me walk you home
and asked me in, coaxed a needle into a groove and the room
crackled alive. Cat Power *Lived in Bars* and we danced
on your tables, djinned tonics, spoke in tongues. *The full meaning
of a language is never translatable into another.* You crushed ice
in your cheek and pressed your winter water fountain
lips against mine, slivering the last ice
into my language with your language
for safekeeping. It's still there, tucked in the attic
in the roof of my mouth. Sometimes it drips
into my saliva, muddling words, making mixed drinks

of my sentences. Months after you moved
I found half a cherry chapstick under my bed, and you lived
at the tip of my tongue for a week. *The full meaning of a language
is never translatable into another.* Someone warned me once
that if I licked a nine-volt it would stick,
and I lapped it up. I'm still reluctant to trust
bus-stop poles in winter, but can't resist
the sriracha nozzle—sharp plastic and sudden heat
pricking like a syringe. When my language
waggles too quickly I trip up in it, start to
slip. *The full meaning of a tongue is never translatable
into another.* Licking my lips
usually fixes that.

After André Kertész's *The Tree, Paris, 1963*

Nine long sawn logs,
strewn like charcoal sticks from a pencil box

across an unfinished drawing
of a riverbank on the Seine. A bridge lops off rooftops

as it crosshatches the skyline, while six men
prod an ashen cloud, perhaps examining the crash site

where an eraser touched down. A tree's trunc-
ated silhouette burlesques the crop

at the top of the photograph, as if
we're witnessing the aftermath

of a flurry of snaps. In the background,
one slim trim branch

slashed
from a tree not far off, as if in imitation,

turns out to be merely
a scratch on the negative.

Waters Above and Waters Below

It took two of us to haul the river out of its box
and wrangle its segments together like vertebrae
or slabs of sidewalk. As rivers go, this one had been
stepped in more than twice, its leisurely ripples and eddies
scuffed with footprints from small armies
of schoolkids. Sweating dust, it slithered
among the geography exhibits like an eel in a sandbox,
writhing with thirst. Have you heard the joke
about all the Trojan Horses hidden inside
dihydrogen monoxide? Hoax or no, the faux-river
waited until we'd locked up and gone home
before triggering its trap. With a tap, tap, tap,
six inches of slush on the science centre roof
slipped through an airlock, a freshet of meltwater
tom-cruising down a ventilation shaft in a rush
for the exhibition hall. It blistered ceiling tiles
like campfire marshmallows, fizzled floodlamps,
liberated a water cooler. It ran sobbing into the arms
of the parched polyurethane riverbed
as if a war had ended. We spent days afterwards
sweeping its tributaries down stairwells,
mopping up and paying tribute, making do
with waterlogged brooms, soggy vending-machine loot
and the PA system's intravenous drip of pop.

Theory of Ghosts

First your hair went white,
now the rest of you. It's as if you woke up
after the operation,
but hamstrung, as if you have to teach yourself
to move and breathe all over again. Your face
looks the same, a little younger even,

more translucent. From your neck down,
things get stranger. Your long, heavy arms
are sodden curtains, bogged with ether,
ectoplasm, entoptic phenomena, whatever
ghosts are composed of. Your abdomen tapers off
like a bloody tooth. Unmoored from beds

and floors, you drift through solid objects,
leave frost on glass.
Within days you learn to pass
for a mote of dust, a moth,
an orchid bloom, and take to hovering
over the shoulders of people you love. They shiver,

close windows, peer at thermostats.
While your grandson practices *Clair de Lune*,
you billow inside the piano and practice
channelling moonlight, flexing
your newfound phosphorescence. Your skin
positively glows, but the mouth you have now

is always open. Wind intones over it
like a bottle, and you spook neighborhood cats
without meaning to. Your daughter's dieffenbachia
withers when you waft too close. You resolve
never to turn into a nuisance, fluttering books
or levitating candlesticks, ooooo-

ooohing. Swivelling into smoke alarms,
light fixtures, the gap above the refrigerator,
you learn to move through the house
without giving anyone chills. You become a connoisseur
of cobwebs, admiring how they graze corners
barely, but with grace. You shudder

to wonder whether your own tethers to this place
might be so tenuous. It's easy to imagine
what little gravity you have left
frazzling thin, leaving you jettisoned
in Earth's silent wake, as the planet unlooms
like a balloon you let go of.

The Observable Universe

So sight, out *sight, which we were obscurely waiting for, was the sight that the others had of us. In one way or another, the great revolution had taken place: all of a sudden, around us, eyes were opening, and corneas and irises and pupils...*

— Italo Calvino, "The Spiral," from *Cosmicomics*

Glory be to augers, drills, and wimbles,
especially those wired into the nervous systems
of dutiful creatures that pierce and perforate
impenetrable surfaces. Oh woodpeckers,
weevils, powderpost beetles, razor clams,
earthworms, termites, and carpenter ants, oh
lockpickers of bark and trespassers of earth,
we praise you through and through and through.
Light has its ways of getting in, but appreciates
an invitation. In today's sermon, we imagine
a beetle tunnelling a hole in the bark of a tree,
hollowing out an acorn-sized log cabin. Pillars
of pinhole-funnelled sunlight converge
upside down on the wall, and coax into focus
the outside world: stippled yellows and greens,
silhouettes of adjacent trees. Our abiding beetle
lounges and lunches, half-watching the camera
obscura like a bored security guard. Maybe its eyes
widen as a menacing shadow lopes past, a moose
or a mammoth. Mostly nothing happens, just light
striking a pose. But in those languid summer hours,
wouldn't pale exposed sapwood begin to darken
in places where light beamed brightest? And if

the trees held still, if the sun took a good long
steady swing, wouldn't a primitive image burn in?
So if you wandered by the next morning
and pried open the bark, you'd find yesterday's forest
fixed there, faintly, in miniature. Or perhaps
you haven't been invented, perhaps this happens
thousands of years before Daguerre or Niépce
or da Vinci, millennia before Adam and Eve,
before beetles even, or earthworms, or trees.
Eons before the first eye fluttered open on Earth,
there were holes in things, and that's all we
need—do you see? Glory be to water dripping!
To falling icicles and freeze-thaw cycles,
to volcanoes and sinkholes, to hailstones,
meteorites, and neutrinos, to those insistent
servants of all that is holey and porous. Praise be
to the gimmick of physics that needled ooze
into eyes. Let there be light in tiny apertures!
Let there be Precambrian photography,
let there be pinhole cameras occurring naturally
on distant planets! An identical trick of the light
is taking place in your skull right now,
twice. Is it so hard to picture?

Coriolis Borealis

If you find yourself lost, try not to walk in circles. A forest
is an aurora of revolving doors, every spruce or fir is
a celestial body that wants you in its orbit. For the first
twenty-four hours, you'd be wise to stay put. Forage
for mushrooms or berries—look for the sulphurous
yellow of the winter chanterelle, *tubaeformis*,
or the simmering wine-red of splendiferous
partridgeberries sweetened by the first frost.
This might require a few exploratory forays,
but try to mark a straight path back and forth, as
it's easy to slip into ellipses. Walk towards the furthest
reliable landmark, taking care to turn back before it's
dark, and be sure to keep warm. One way to start a fire is
to grind two splints of wood together with enough force
that they smoke and spark, over a pile of moss, coniferous
needles, lichen, pocket lint, anything flammable and fibrous.
Find shelter, stay dry, and try to sleep for at least
a few hours. Never wander after dark, nights are formless
and haunted by wrong turns. Focus. Have a goal to aim for, just
as the sun rises in the east and strikes out for the west.
Sometimes, the best you can do is prepare for the worst.

The Day After the Best Before

The clouds over Halifax are the insipid pink of Canada
on old National Geographic maps, fringed red
like freezer-burnt meat. A sunburned crowd stares
at the harbour as if holding open a refrigerator door,
as if we're trying to decide how hungry we are. Bare shoulders
clink like bottles. It's still a half-hour until the fireworks,
and the clouds glisten like iridescent ham, as if they might be
going bad. The sun a dim bulb above a glass shelf. A cover band's
Sweet Home Alabama drifts from a pub as a waiter folds a tablecloth
like a flag. A woman waves across the crowd with oven mitts
shaped like lobster claws. A man presses a paper cup
against his cheek, smudging a maple leaf. A flare of colour
over Dartmouth is too far off to be the city's fireworks,
but it's enough that boats slow and switch off
deck lights, bystanders tighten grips
on stroller handles and cameras. For twenty minutes, the crowd
grumbles like a stomach. When the sky finally explodes
it's a quick forgettable pleasure, like remembering
there's a tub of ice cream in the freezer. It's easy to imagine
that what everyone secretly desires is the raw astoundment
of a mushroom cloud. Like opening your refrigerator
to find the processed ham replaced by the smell of putrid flesh
and the sprawling five-tongued nightmare of a corpse
flower, *Rafflesia*, an insatiable eldritch orifice transplanted
from the jungles of Borneo to your kitchen. Something worth
witnessing. Something strange enough that you're forced
to ask yourself what you're really hungry for.

In Print

Vuillard's Interiors

Alive inside the oeuvre of Édouard Vuillard
(the way a tremor is alive in a heart) we move
without moving (the way a needle moves through a quilt)
from *Sunlit Interior* to *Large Interior with Six Persons*,
to *Figures in an Interior*, to *In the Waiting Room*,
swept up (the way dust is swept up) in a series
of savourless gestures. Notice how light, too,
has become alluvial, collecting along edges,
gossamering in corners. In every room
women come and go, attending to desks and pianos,
turning their backs to windows. Passing through
(the way sunlight passes through) the verdant curtains
that pass for walls, we strike out for farther interiors,
voyaging up rivers of ivy without lifting a finger
except to rub our eyes. In *Interior*, a gardener
moonlighting as a decorator has installed a beehive
in the chandelier, to cross-pollinate tablecloths
with curtains and walls. Notice the buzz in the air,
a sonata played entirely *niente*. We'll pause a moment
for a little experiment—look, here. Now throw
(as a magic lantern throws!) your eyes out of focus
until flowers diffuse from their walls, and the room
dissolves into something more luminous, voluminous,
the bloomy nebulae of muddled distances. Roaming
from salon to salon in such a fugue, some visitors
have caught sight of Vuillard himself, quavering
beneath the music of a farther room, or looming

where there used to be a door. Today we'll settle
(the way that dust settles) for the artist's signature—
have you spotted it yet, smirking like a fork
on the floor? Burglarious gardens press against
every window, and the cutlery drawers
are full of orchids. In *Interior with Pink Wallpaper*
the very atmosphere throbs with rosehips and bulbs
so that breathing is like bobbing for apples.
We'll come up for air in *Entrance to the Garden*,
recuperate in wicker chairs, let a lush breeze
rinse fragrances from our lungs. Our tour ends
(as a silence ends) here, where we've barely begun.

View of the Narrows

Some days the horizon is roughed in
with a paint roller, some days
a pencil and ruler.

The hills on the south side of the harbour
just floating there, without the clothespin
of a tiny stone tower.

Walking on Moss

collaged fragments from Audubon's *Labrador Journal* of 1833

This evening I went on shore with the captain
for exercise, and enough have I had. More than once
I thought I should give up from weariness.
Treading over the spongy moss of Labrador
is a task beyond conception until tried—with every step
the foot sinks into a deep, soft cushion

which closes over it. A velvet growth of vegetation
that would astound any European garden,
yet not a cubic foot of soil! Granite, granite, granite,
moss, moss, moss, and nothing but granite and moss
of thousands of species. Gray-clothed rocks, heaped
and thrown together in fantastical groups, huge masses

hanging on minor ones as if about to roll themselves
into the depths of the sea beneath. We sank in moss
nearly up to our middles—to reach a bare rock
is delightful, and quite a relief. Walking over
the stubborn, dwarfish shrubbery makes me think
that as I go I tread down the very forests

of Labrador. Butterflies flitting over snow-banks,
probing dwarf flowerets pushing their tender stems
from the thick bed of moss, and trees like so many mops
of wiry composition. Trudging through the great bog
was so fatiguing that we frequently lay down to rest;
our sinews became cramped. Saw not a quadruped.

Somewhere Near Hodderville

What's the word for a group
of knackered pocketknives heaved up
on a beach, gleaming and googly-eyed,
each twerking their single flimsy hinge,
agape, agog, and rubbernecking
as if, having escaped first a factory
and then some sardine-can
container ship, they can't quite
believe this is the end of it, twitching
turning to flip-flopping turning to
thrashing themselves breathless,
self-flagellating to within an inch
of their lives, which were only
a few inches to begin with, a crescendo
of the sound of one hand clapping, a swell
of plentiful disappointments palpitating
and graspable, a wriggling feast
of spent shotgun-and-sausage
casings? Capelin.

Portable Keyhole

after Alan Gillis

That scene in *Rear Window* when Stella asks,
Mind if I use that portable keyhole? and our voyeur

hands her his tool of the trade, his trusty blade,
his spyglass, his shadow catcher, his body snatcher,
his one-way mirror, his black box theatre,
the sharpest arrow in his quiver,

his eye for an eye, his thirty-six-shooter,
his uber-neighbour-ogler, his super-duper-snooper,
his laser pistol, lightsaber, cloak and dagger, crown
and sceptre, his male gazer, his spotlight and interrogation chamber,

his machine that lies both always and never, his hocus
focus, his magnum opus, his crystal ball of confirmation
bias, his perfect witness, his look-what-I-got-for-Christmas,
his gizmo with machismo, his gear acquisition syndrome,

his paparazzo, his photon torpedo, his supervillain monocle,
his jeepers peeper, his housecreeper, his finder-and-keeper,
his grin reaper, his crowd-pleaser, his eyeballistic missile
launcher, his play-by-play announcer, his you-should-smile-more,

his satellite slash lunar lander slash space invader,
his where-no-man-has-gone-before, his fantasies of interplanetary
warfare, his historical record, his prism, his prison,
his surveillance system, his shut-up-and-listen,

his panopticon, his bag of popcorn, and says,
Go ahead, just as long as you tell me what you're looking at.

Some Kind of Understanding (3)

A squiggle ripples, a scurry
wriggles, a waggle squirrels
along a wire.

—

Having cantered millions of miles
through void, cloud, glass, and curtain,
sunlight is flummoxed by linoleum.

—

A mouse in the ceiling between floors,
as if I'd knocked on my upstairs neighbour's door
and asked to borrow a cup of wilderness.

Boats and Ships

I was today years old when I learned that *boat*
is not interchangeable with *ship*. I've often thought of them
as synonyms, boat playing second fiddle
to ship's violin, or ship is to boat as dove is to
pigeon. Merely a class distinction—no one drifts
for weeks in a lifeship, no one sips cocktails
on a cruise boat. But nope! Colloquially, the consensus is:
ships can carry boats, but boats can't carry ships
(thus ship is to boat as bowl is to spoon). Questions remain
among shipspotters and prescriptivists, who quibble over
square-rigged crafts with at least three masts (ships),
whether the vessel is ever brought onto land (only boats),
or how a watercraft's centre of gravity determines the way
it leans when it turns. As it turns out (ship), this soon turns in
(boat) to rearranging deck chairs (Titanic), and I sink
back to gutsier instincts: to *boat* is to transport yourself,
to *ship* usually to send something else. Ships imply
a certain distance, while boats hew closer to home
and to the human body, their ribs exposed. Boats sail,
ships tow, ships tell, boats show. You can only row
a boat. You can only make a ship of the tongue, or ship
under the radar into something more comfortable,
or ship the surly bonds of Earth (no one blasts off
in a spaceboat). Are boats blown to bits
the same as ships smashed to pieces? Ask Theseus,
or the nearest thesaurus. Boat is to ship
as craft is to art—both only as close as heart is to heart.

Ode on a Rotten Potato

O malignant tuber,

O hemeteorrhoid,

O pomme de terrible,

O unholy hand grenade,

O botched ophthalmoscopy,

O asteroid belch,

O malodorous opal,

O putrid petri dish,

O ungobbledygook,

O subterranean homesick blues,

O leprous embryo,

O primordial bruise,

O morbid geode,

O psychopompeii,

O involuntary vodka,

O crudest of crudités,

O murmurous haunt of flies, allow me

to feed deep, deep upon your peerless eyes.

Merchant Vessels

Ferry, ferry, ferry, as if you changed your mind
halfway through saying *farewell*, as if you blew a kiss
into a headwind, as if a love letter, misaddressed,
bounced from North Sydney to Port aux Basques,
to North Sydney, to Port aux Basques, an accidental
twenty-four-year courtship. The MV *Caribou*,
the MV *Joseph and Clara Smallwood. Emm vee*,
not *most valuable* but *merchant vessel*, a mellifluous vintage
of a phrase, with hints of *mussel, kestrel, sessile, fossil*,
of *fissile*, a piece of wood split along the grain,
of *ventricle, vascular*, steam pluming
from smokestacks as thick as butchers' wrists, of *vestige*,
every knot in a plank gripping a memory of how it felt
when wind rushed through a forest. *Merchant*,
mercenary, mercurial, mercy. The Caribou and *Smallwood*
were retired from service in 2011, and mistakenly
(Marine Atlantic claimed) sold to a company in Alang, India
for shipbreaking. *According to the UN,*
209 workers were killed in accidents in Alang
between 1996 and 2003. Whistle, the shrill
of a kettle threatening hell, *visceral*. The opposition's
environment critic called it utterly reprehensible:
We shouldn't be sending our problems overseas.
We're talking about kids in India breaking down
that vessel.

Vessel, vessel, two esses
zipped together, a switchblade of breath
slicing open a purse. *S,* the hiss
and shapelessness of misfired fireworks,
indecisive rivers, a welding torch. *Vessel*
insinuates a shell, a nest, a bowl, a fist;
anything that simultaneously holds and is held. The MV *Hopedale,*
in 1984, guttered on fire for thirty-six hours before going under.
The records say, *sank at berth.* Seven weeks later she was raised
to be scuttled twelve nautical miles south. The SS *Caribou*
left Sydney in October 1942 and never saw land again.
Miss Fitzpatrick, the stewardess, passed the remark
about not expecting to get much rest that night
as there were several small children on board. At 3:40 a.m.
a U-boat torpedoed the *Caribou* on her starboard side.
She sank five minutes later, taking 136 with her.
Fifty-seven were military personnel and forty-nine were civilians.
A fifteen-month-old from Halifax was the only one
of eleven children to survive the sinking. SOS
because it was easy to Morse, not because
it stood for anything.

Berrypickers in Bauline

Margaret calls them *toadberries* because they jump
right into her bucket. My uncle calls them *salmonellaberries*,
but doesn't like to talk about it. Winston calls them
starberries because you find more as your eyes adjust.

Virginia calls them *can'ttell'emapartidgeberries*
because she always gets them mixed up. Doug named them
submarineberries because they do evasive manoeuvres
in the brush. Candice calls them *blushberries* because

their skin catches fire at her touch. Jane calls them *hangoverberries*,
and adds handfuls to her homebrew. Rosie calls them
christmaslightberries because once one goes bad,
they all do. Mandy calls them *macbethberries* because

she can never wash their stains off her hands. My dad
calls them *doomberries* because he was there with my uncle,
and never again. Alex calls them *sarahberries*, claims
they're the colour of her eyes. Sarah calls them *bittenberries*

because they're never as thick as the flies. Laura calls them
pallberries, says their leaves look like little white gloves.
Tom calls them *traveling wilberries*, because they taste
like all the best berries at once. Wanda calls them *swanberries*

since they're sort of like gooseberries, but not. Dermot
thinks of them as *alienberries* because sometimes
hideous bugs burst out. Sandy calls them *tambourineberries*
because of the sound when they jangle around. Eileen says

they're *minimumwageberries* because you only get eight bucks
a gallon. Aunt Winnie, bless her heart, calls them *waxberries*
and swears they don't have a taste. Kim's always called them
Baulineberries, because she's only ever found them

in that one place.

Suomi Snowball

The lackadaisical *tsk, tsk, tsk* of a distant electric fence. Hämeen-kyrö's neighbourly umlauts. Reindeer lichen's diminutive fingers brushing mine. Moss grazing on raindrops. Snot that drips on my touchscreen and misfocuses the camera, ice crystals blooming into costume jewellery. The sharp resinous scent of sap on my wrist. Frost, which every night reupholsters the yard in shaggier splinters of glass. Two whooper swans on a one-euro coin. The metallic tang of salmiakki ice cream.

A snapped bootlace. A replacement I pilfer from the lost and found. A mushroom I take a selfie with, nudging my phone beneath its cap. The Soviet opera glasses I find at a consignment shop, toylike yellow plastic belying bright clear lenses. Air bubbles like stacked saucers in the frozen lake. Five euros' worth of paper-wrapped smoked trout from a stall outside the supermarket. Moss-icicles. My fingers, numb from manipulating camera dials in clammy November air. A lens flare like the ghost of an apple.

Dime-a-dozen sunbursts of lichen bespangling bark. Tove Jansson, crowned in wildflowers and swimming, on the cover of her selected short stories. Magpies like winged Nanaimo bars. Speckled birds I don't know the names of, flitting and conniving through a field of tattered reeds. The sauna's milky orb light, a manageable moon. A mauzy farmhouse seen through opera glasses. A bent, dead sun-flower like a burnt-out lamp. My ice-encrusted footprints from the day before, which I follow to see where they go.

A bronze plaque commemorating Frans Eemil Sillanpää, who donated his Nobel medal to be melted down to aid Finland in the Winter War. A huge motionless hare. Two spooked deer like whisked handkerchiefs. The drawling hiss of steam when someone pours fresh water on heated stones. A rowboat frozen in place beside the lake. Folk music on Yle Radio Suomi flooding the car. A cluster of colourful beehives beside a field, each capped with a single large rock. A squabbling gaggle of swans, a nebulous spatter of white against fog. Their detuned symphony, larger than themselves.

A tall pine sentinelling a grove of smokey birch. The snowy parking lot outside the public sauna that I scurry across wearing a towel. The icewater lake that instantly slurps every nerve in my body out through my fingertips. Frost-roughened fields like animal hide unrolled across the earth, stubbled with cut wheat and long ploughlines that make it hard to walk. Morning mist like an underpainting. A swath of forest unfurling through a half-scraped passenger window.

Orion's dot dot dot coaxed closer through opera glasses. A cloudless night sky glistering with more stars as my vision attunes. A quiet train ride from Helsinki to Tampere in late afternoon dusk. The salmon sunrise on that last morning at Arteles. Two transatlantic flights, there and back again. The second heavier than the first.

Mundy Pond

Any place on the trail is as good as another
to draw a map of Mundy Pond. Just take a pencil
and throw it as far as you can. Its splash
sketches the contour of the water, widening
to include the trail you're standing on, then the street
surrounding that. See how concentric bands
bloom to suggest the city limits, peninsula,
island, ocean, planet—each circumference
graciously offering another, like a teacup
resting perfectly in its saucer? Once the innermost
contour expands to reach shore, our map tatters
into territory, and we find ourselves,
like Borges, back in the deserts of the west
end of St. John's. Now try it again, this time
imagining each ripple a more powerful lens—
our splash begins as a satellite photo, then furrows
through bird's-eye, bug's-eye, and tadpole's-eye views.
It ripples into the woodgrain of the pencil you threw,
into the carbon atoms at its core, into proton, electron,
quark, until one last lingering ring gestures towards
something we haven't imagined enough to
name. Something so profoundly mundane
they should call it Mundy Pond.

Bus

Wiper swish, wiper swish. Low voices muffled
by a pothole's *harrumph harrumph*. Sniffles.
The stifled tambourine of someone
tipping back a box of mints. Beneath it all,
an internal combustion engine's
interminable drum solo. I open my eyes
and it's only been thirty-eight minutes.
The clock above the windshield glows 08:08.
A voice wobbles up the aisle like a ball
of yarn: *This'll be my first sober birthday
in nineteen years.* The man tells a stranger
he plans to retrain for the offshore. *What do you do?*
Me? Same as everyone stuck in this aquarium
for ten hours: I pretzel and unpretzel
my legs, crinkle chip bags, tap a screen
to toggle between whimsy and inklings
of doomsday. A Guardian article
admonishes about the "windshield phenomenon"—
how insects no longer blitzkrieg drivers
with the intensity we remember. I gaze past
a hurtling vacuum of black spruce
at the Come By Chance oil refinery.
I watch my phone battery drain away
searching for satellites, for wi-fi,
for anything. The clock glows 09:13. I blink
and it's snowing and the clock glows
09:39. The bus's upholstery pattern

might best be described as velociraptor-claw
tsunami. The gutter of traumatized planet
on either side of the highway might best be described
as ahead by a century. Scrub, scruff, scree,
a bowling lane of toppled evergreens, hubcaps
and coffee cups, herbicides, makeshift shrines
to moose-vehicle accidents. A passenger
twirls a coil of turquoise hair between her fingers
as an enormous blue waterslide ammonites into the sky
behind the Splash-n-Putt gas pumps. The clock
glows 10:01. Birches are stodgy lightning bolts
in a primordial soup of spruce. Yesterday my housemate
told me *I bussed across the island in a blizzard once*
and they gave us a police escort, closing the highway
behind us as we went. Wiper swish. The bus attendant
slots in a DVD and an orchestra of jittery screens
crescendos into car chase after car chase. A siren wails,
a kid in the front joins in. *Humans threaten one million*
species with extinction. How many is a million?
A thousand thousand, a hundred hundred hundred,
tens and tens and tens and tens and tens and tens
of species. We are closing the world behind us
as we go. The clock glows 10:43. The clock
glows 11:58. The windshield gleams.

Logbook

A madeleine dipped in lime-flower tea
blooms rings in a cup. Proust takes a sip
and backflips four centuries to a Florentine
workshop where Leonardo, turning wood
on a lathe, invents dendrochronology
by mistake. Later, in the film *La Jetée*,
a time-traveller points at a cross-section
of redwood, then moves his finger beyond
its orbit, reckoning where a ring will form
in the year when he's born. Circling back,
we find the scene rooted in one from *Vertigo*—
a woman possessed by the past lingers
at a redwood slab, strumming its rings,
muttering *Somewhere in here I was born,*
and here I died—it was only a moment for you—
you took no notice. Thrown for a loop,
her companion cries: *Madeleine!*

After André Kertész's *Central Park Boat Basin,*
New York, 1944

An unfinished picture, half-fished
from a tray of developer, spills forth
a tree upside-drowning in rainwater
and a double exposure: some species

of minotaur, half-man half-schooner,
slouching towards a boathouse or bathysphere.
Charon, or one of his psychopomp coworkers
trimmed to the bones: a pair of legs sutured

to seven sharp pieces of silver. Only strangers
ever get any younger. Kertész, at ninety,
asked why he was still taking photographs,
replied: *I'm still hungry.*

Tinkers Point Path

When the tip of my pencil snaps, I think of
Tinkers Point Path, that stub of stubborn grass
where the trail cracked off into blackened rocks
like burnt shipwrecks, and a stern wind
clipped the sharpest branches from our words
before we could finish them. *Someth abou*
thi pla maes me wan to li dow, you shouted,
so we did, side-by-side on the stubble, salt spray
sandpapering our noses. I'd been reading about Turner's
Snow Storm – Steam-Boat off a Harbour's Mouth,
how the painter had asked to be strapped
to the steamboat mast as it swayed,
swung there for four hours as the ice
scrimshawed the ivory of his eyes,
then lambasted his canvas until it howled
the same howl. *I did not paint it*
to be understood, he later claimed, *but wished*
to show what such a scene was like. Turning
my head, I noticed the cliff-edge cuffed
in wild rosehips like a spatter of dried blood,
having clung to their masts somehow
all winter. You lay beside me, whittling
silence into fine argument. *I was lashed*
for four hours, and I did not expect to escape,
but I felt bound to record it if I did. But no one
had any business to like the picture.

Woodstove

Sprung a latch
and the door swung open. Stuck my nose in
that blackened cave where images spark
and flicker, shunted a used-up spool
to one side of the dark, jimmied a fresh cylinder
into the sprocket til it caught. Took a breath,
blew the dust out, clamped the door
tight. Leaned close, squinting though glass
at new-sharpened light.
                        Liked the lick of it
so I camped there all night, burning through
roll after roll, dreaming
of Lascaux. Nothing to show for it now
but cold, every frigging frame
overexposed.

Notes

"A Profusion of Handsome Japanese Papers" contains lines from a Calvin & Hobbes comic, and "Moss" the chorus from Sylvia Plath's "Mushrooms." In "North Head Trail," the word *galefilero* is from *The Dictionary of Newfoundland English* and means "a jaunt; a rambling walk or ride just for the sake of breaking restraint." "Olbers' Paradox, or Sunglasses at Night" paraphrases Edgar Allen Poe's essay "Eureka."

"Tickling the Scar" was written during the early months of the pandemic and quotes several news articles from CBC and the Montreal Gazette, particularly the Gazette's Aaron Derfel. The title of "Seeing Is Forgetting the Name of the Thing One Sees" is an aphorism attributed to Paul Valéry. "The full meaning of a language" line in "With Tongue" is from Maurice Merleau-Ponty's *Phenomenology of Perception*.

A few snippets from T.S. Eliot's "The Love Song of J. Alfred Prufrock" are lounging around "Vuillard's Interiors." "Portable Keyhole" was inspired by Alan Gillis's "The Lad," from his book *Hawks and Doves*. "Boats and Ships" was written in response to the work of sculptor K MacLean for Craft NB's project *Atlantic Vernacular*. "Ode on a Rotten Potato" borrows from Keats's "Ode on Melancholy." The David Milne passage is edited for brevity—I found it in a *Canadian Art* article by Sarah Milroy. "Merchant Vessels" contains quotations (also slightly paraphrased) from a CBC article ("Marine Atlantic ferry disposal outrages MP") and from William J. Lundrigan's account of the sinking of the SS *Caribou*. "Mundy Pond" references Jorge Luis Borges's "On Exactitude in Science." The quotation in "Tinkers Point Path" is J.M.W. Turner in conversation with John Ruskin.

Acknowledgements

Earlier versions of several of these poems have appeared in *The Malahat Review*, *The Fiddlehead*, *PRISM international*, *subTerrain*, *Arc*, CBC Books, *Newfoundland Quarterly*, *Riddle Fence*, *Cartwheel*, and *Paragon*. Many thanks to everyone who has given my work a home.

I would never have finished this collection without the support of ArtsNL, the Writers' Alliance of Newfoundland & Labrador, and Memorial University's Department of English. An earlier version of *Optic Nerve* was awarded the 2017 NLCU Fresh Fish Award for Emerging Writers. I wrote a handful of these poems during a writing residency in Brigus as part of the 2018 Cox & Palmer SPARKS Creative Writing Award, and wrote "Frost" and "Suomi Snowball" while at Arteles Creative Centre in Finland. "Tickling the Scar" won the 2020 CBC Poetry Prize, "Merchant Vessels" won *The Malahat Review*'s 2021 Open Season Award, and "The Day After the Best Before" won *The Fiddlehead*'s 2018 Ralph Gustafson Prize for Best Poem.

No poet could ask for more perceptive, encouraging, and scrupulous editors than Barry Dempster and Sue Sinclair—I'm incredibly grateful to have been fortunate enough to work with both of you. Thanks a million to everyone at Brick Books, especially the endlessly helpful and understanding Alayna Munce. My gratitude also to superstar designer Marijke Friesen, and to artist Jon McNaught for the use of his exquisite lithograph.

I feel particularly grateful to have been mentored in 2015 by the brilliant Mark Callanan, through WANL's Emerging Writers Mentorship Program, just when this book was starting to take shape. Thank you, Mark! So many of these poems are much sharper because of your keen pocketknife brain.

Thanks also to Don McKay, Rob Finley, Lisa Moore, Mary Dalton, everyone in my writing groups, and the wonderful writing community in St. John's. Deep thanks to Stephanie McKenzie and Randall Maggs, who were so encouraging when I was just getting started. And thanks of course to Mom and Dad, for everything.

NEWFOUNDLAND AND LABRADOR ARTS COUNCIL

Matthew Hollett is a writer and photographer in St. John's, Newfoundland (Ktaqmkuk). A graduate of the MFA program at NSCAD University, his work explores landscape and memory through photography, writing, and walking. Hollett won the 2020 CBC Poetry Prize for "Tickling the Scar," a poem about walking the Lachine Canal during the early days of the pandemic. He has previously been awarded the NLCU Fresh Fish Award for Emerging Writers, *The Fiddlehead*'s Ralph Gustafson Prize for Best Poem, and VANL-CARFAC's Critical Eye Award for art writing. His first book, *Album Rock* (2018), is a work of creative nonfiction and poetry investigating a curious photo taken in the 1850s by Paul-Émile Miot, one of the first photographers to visit Newfoundland.

Instagram: @matthewhollett
www.matthewhollett.com